the

ZEN

book

Hay House Titles
of Related Interest

Everyday Positive Thinking, by Louise L. Hay

Everyday Wisdom, by Dr. Wayne W. Dyer

Feng Shui Dos & Taboos for Health & Well-Being, by Angi Ma Wong

Goddess Guidance Oracle Cards, by Doreen Virtue, Ph.D.

*How to Get from Where You Are
to Where You Want to Be,* by Cheri Huber

Meditations, by Sylvia Browne

Simple Things, by Jim Brickman, with Cindy Pearlman

Wisdom of the Heart, by Alan Cohen

Zen Cards, by Daniel Levin

and

Journals, Notecards, and Candles:
Zen, Angels, Power Thought, Healing, and *Love and Relationships*

All the above are available
at your local bookstore, or may be ordered by visiting:
Hay House USA: **www.hayhouse.com**
Hay House Australia: **www.hayhouse.com.au**
Hay House UK: **www.hayhouse.co.uk**
Hay House South Africa: **orders@psdprom.co.za**

the ZEN book

Daniel Levin

LIFE *Styles*

HAY HOUSE, INC.

Carlsbad, California

London • Sydney • Johannesburg

Vancouver • Hong Kong

Published and distributed in the United States by: Hay House, Inc., P.O. Box 5100, Carlsbad, CA 92018-5100 • *Phone:* (760) 431-7695 or (800) 654-5126 • *Fax:* (760) 431-6948 or (800) 650-5115 • www.hayhouse.com • *Published and distributed in Australia by:* Hay House Australia Pty. Ltd., 18/36 Ralph St., Alexandria NSW 2015 • *Phone:* 612-9669-4299 • *Fax:* 612-9669-4144 • www.hayhouse.com.au • *Published and distributed in the United Kingdom by:* Hay House UK, Ltd. • Unit 62, Canalot Studios • 222 Kensal Rd., London W10 5BN • *Phone:* 44-20-8962-1230 • *Fax:* 44-20-8962-1239 • www.hayhouse.co.uk • *Published and distributed in the Republic of South Africa by:* Hay House SA (Pty), Ltd., P.O. Box 990, Witkoppen 2068 • *Phone/Fax:* 27-11-706-6612 • orders@psdprom.co.za • *Distributed in Canada by:* Raincoast • 9050 Shaughnessy St., Vancouver, B.C. V6P 6E5 • *Phone:* (604) 323-7100 • *Fax: (604) 323-2600*

Design: Amy Rose Szalkiewicz
All photographs and/or copyright: Jerome Alfred Johnson, 2005

Library of Congress Control Number: 2004116119

Hardcover ISBN 13: 987-1-4019-0875-1
Hardcover ISBN 10: 1-4019-0875-6
Tradepaper ISBN 13: 978-1-4019-0701-3
Tradepaper ISBN 10: 1-4019-0701-6

08 07 06 05 4 3 2 1
1st printing, August 2005

Printed in Thailand by Imago

To Elisa,
who has taught me
more than she will
ever comprehend.

Contents

Introduction

I remember being told a story. Although I'd heard it a thousand times before, as I listened to it this time it changed my life. Have you ever seen that black-and-white drawing that, when viewed one way, looks like a vase, while if you look at it differently, it appears to be two faces in profile? When you see one of the images, you can't see the other. This is what happened to me upon hearing that one story again . . . for the first time.

I also recall hearing "God is love" for the first time. I thought, *That is so beautiful.* Later, I heard "God is love" again, and I couldn't believe that I'd never understood it before. And when I heard it yet again years later, it was entirely new and wonderful, and the realization was as if I'd never heard it. Each time I heard "God is love," it went deeper into me—and it was as if I was peeling layers off of myself to ultimately discover anew my innermost being.

My hope in writing down the sayings and stories in this book is that you'll discover the "Zen Mind," the mind that sees all things for the first time. Each time you read a story, it will be as if you've never read it before. And each time, the meaning of the story will enter you anew.

A drop of water that continuously drips on a rock eventually makes a hole; similarly, these are sayings and stories that, when read over time, peel away the layers of who we think we "should" be and almost imperceptibly allow us to become who we are.

The stories in this book comes from many different places. Many of them I've read in books, others have been told to me by my teachers, and still others are from the great religious traditions. Regardless, they all have the power to change perceptions by offering a new way of looking at something we've seen a thousand times before.

When we're ready to see, we see. When we're ready to learn, we remember. This, then, is a book of memories. It isn't meant to teach, but rather to remind us of what we already know.

I share with you now one simple story that changed my life.

A man walked into a Shiva temple [Shiva is the Hindu God of destruction—the destroyer of bad habits and so forth]. In the middle of the room was a lingam [a phalliclike stone]. The man sat down on the floor and put his feet up on the lingam.

The priest of the temple rushed in and asked, "Don't you know what a sin you've just done? No one can put their feet on such a holy shrine! The punishment for such an act is eternity in hell."

The man, humble in his way, answered, "Please accept my apology, for I did not know that what I did was wrong. Can you please place my feet somewhere where God won't be offended?"

Immediately, the priest took the man's feet off the stone and threw them to the ground. To the man's surprise, before his feet could touch the ground, another Shiva lingam appeared to catch them. Not believing his eyes, the priest again threw the man's feet from the second lingam to the floor. And once again, a lingam appeared to catch the man's feet.

This time the humble man, with a glimmer in his eye, asked the priest to place his feet where God did not exist. At that, the priest bowed to the feet of this holy man and apologized.

The holy man replied, "There is no place where God is not."

When I heard this, it struck me that if God is everywhere and in everything, what I needed to do was see the perfection that already existed in all things. Nothing needed changing—everything had perfection already in it. I realized that my pain comes from wanting things to be other than they are. When I accept things as they are, I'm completely happy.

In Zen, the saying *Wabi Sabi* means "the perfectly imperfect." Since nothing in this world is perfect, the practice of Wabi Sabi is seeing that which is perfect in all of life's imperfections.

May all sentient beings be released from their suffering and find happiness.

Be
yourself.

You are so beautiful. Never before in creation has there been anyone exactly like you.

You are unique in the whole universe—what could be more beautiful than that?

When we accept
ourselves completely,

enlightenment happens.

The teacher walked around the room

and told the disciples that they'd all be free. One student was told he'd be free this lifetime, another in the next lifetime, and so on. When he got to his closest disciple, the teacher told him that he'd be free in 100,000 lifetimes. As the other students cringed in pain, they didn't see that this certain disciple was up and dancing. When they noticed, they came to him and asked, "Didn't you hear what the teacher said—it will take you 100,000 more lifetimes to be free?"

The student replied, "Didn't *you* hear what he said? In 100,000 lifetimes I will be *free!*"

At that moment, the teacher came over and slapped this disciple on the chest, and he immediately became enlightened. The teacher wanted the others to see the devotion of a true disciple.

You are perfect exactly as you are.

With all your flaws and problems,
there's no need to change anything.
All you need to change is the thought
that you have to change.

A beautiful way
to pray for others

is to breathe in their suffering and breathe out your joy.
With each exhalation, feel that you're expelling their pain.
With each inhalation, feel happiness filling the
space created by pulling out their pain.
(Do this as a means to end your own suffering, too.)

A judge came to a teacher

and asked him how he could give up so much for the sake of his beliefs. The teacher said, "A thief broke into my house and while he was there, he dropped something that he'd stolen from another house that was of more value than all that he'd taken from me. I'm wondering what I should do: Should I try to return the jewel that the thief left?"

The judge said, "Foolish man, keep what you have! It's of more value, so don't try to return it."

The teacher then looked the judge in the eye and said, "Follow your own advice. The things of this world are meaningless when you've found the source of true happiness. What the thief left me is far greater than what he took away."

In that moment, the judge became a student of the teacher.

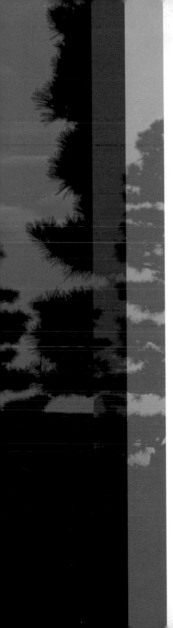

The only problem
that ever exists

is not accepting things the way they are.
This is the cause of all suffering.

Practice
being nothing—

no thing.
In doing so,
you'll become
everything.

A Zen monk was invited

to the monastery of another religion to discuss religious practice. He told them that if they'd meditate and live mindfully in all that they do, enlightenment would surely come. One of the other monks there said, "But teacher, we live a simple life of prayer without effort, waiting for the grace of God to come and illuminate us."

The Zen monk replied simply, "In the practice of Zen, we believe that God has already done his share. All that awaits doing is our part."

Watch the clouds. . . .

As they pass unruffled over peaks and valleys, they're not elated by the peaks, nor bored by the valleys. That is the Zen mind: neither elated nor bored, but rather always at peace.

Sentient beings everywhere want the same thing:

to get out of pain and be happy.
The delusion of this world is that
we think we're the only ones
who have pain—we imagine that
everyone else's life is going great.
When we realize that we're all the
same, that we all have pain and
suffering, then we see the world
with the utmost compassion.

A student had an amazing revelation that truly touched his soul.

He awoke to find that God is everywhere. And as he wandered the streets, he smiled as he saw his beloved in all things. Before he knew it, he was walking right in the path of an elephant being driven by a man who had lost control. The elephant was running right toward the student! *No fear,* he thought. *God is in me, God is in the elephant.*

The driver of the elephant was now screaming at the top of his lungs: "Wild elephant! Get out of the way!" The student kept telling himself, *God is in me, God is in the ele*—BAM! Before he could finish thinking the word *elephant,* he was struck down by the uncontrollable beast. The student awoke in the hospital days later, saying he didn't understand: If God was everywhere, how could this have happened?

And his friend said, "God was also in the elephant driver, telling you to get out of the way."

The river flows, the mountain remains motionless.

The river can't remain still, nor can the mountain flow. Is one right or wrong? Our *dharma* (duty) is to do what's ours to do, not to be like others.

Watch the caterpillar become a butterfly:

Does he not transform? Is it because of his effort that this happens? Why then do we think that we're responsible for changing ourselves?

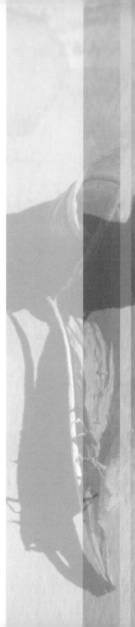

Run after the things of this world,

and quite often what you seek so desperately runs away from you. Covet nothing, crave nothing, and celebrate whatever comes—this is the way of contentment.

Perfection isn't found in everything going right,

but rather in accepting the beauty of what's happening moment to moment.

There's a story of three men in search of enlightenment.

Their teacher told them that he'd take them to a field to visit a wall that they wouldn't be able to get over on their own. Yet on the other side of the wall was everything they were seeking. After their teacher left, the three men promised each other that they wouldn't go over unless all three went together.

When they got to the wall, the first man climbed on the backs of the other two, stood on top of the wall, and said to the others, "It's so beautiful." And without hesitation, he jumped over to the other side.

The remaining two looked at each other and exclaimed, "I can't believe he did that! We made a pact that we'd only go over together." Nevertheless, the second man ended up doing the same to the third man.

In shock, the third man returned to town to tell his story. He ended up bringing thousands to the wall, helping them see the other side, and then assisting them up and over. He sacrificed all that he sought so that others could have what they wanted. At the end of his days, his students hoisted him up on their backs and helped *him* get to the top of the wall. As he peered over, he saw in an instant why his brothers all jumped the second they saw what was there, but then he looked at all the people on this side of the wall—all that he could still bring over—and he jumped back to the side from which he came. In that moment the wall dropped, and all that were in the field with him became enlightened.

For some, their work is to help others, but for others, their work is simply to change themselves. Neither is right or wrong, better or worse.

Practice kindness,

not because it's right or because someone tells you to,
but because it will bring you happiness.

No matter who we are—

doctor, lawyer, prostitute, or thief—we're all the same.
We fear the same things, long for the same intimacy,
and want to love and be loved.

The waves go in and out, crash, and remain still.

This is the ebb and flow of life. Everything is constantly
changing: Excitement is followed by quiet, which is followed
by upheaval, which is followed by peace. Become whatever's
happening, always content to be with what is.

*Lose a
flower
and you can
easily find
another,*

lose integrity and you'll wander
for some time until you find it again.

The monks in the Zendo decided that they were going to plant a garden.

They bought seeds of the most beautiful flowers they could find, planted them, and watered the soil, taking care to give the flower bed the perfect amount of sunlight and water. They would have the most beautiful garden ever!

One by one, the flowers grew, and each was more beautiful than the next. The monks were so proud of what they'd grown. A villager came by, saw their garden, and noticed that flowering weeds were all over the place. When he asked the monks why they hadn't pulled the weeds, they replied, "Because we never saw them."

No matter what people say about you,

know who you are.
Their blame can't injure you,
nor can their praise elevate you.
You are what you are;
nothing anyone can say can change that.

The holy man
was glorified by the whole town

as a being who lived his life with purity and dignity. In the village was a beautiful young girl who resided with her family next door. When her parents found out that she was pregnant, they were livid and demanded to know who had done this to her. She refused to tell them, but after much time and harassment, she finally revealed that the father of her child was the holy man. Outraged, the parents went to tell him what had happened. He looked at them and said, "Is that so?"

When the baby was born, he was brought to the holy man, who by now had totally lost his reputation. The baby's grandparents demanded that he care for the child, which he did without complaint. Finding everything the baby needed, he happily took care of him. Some time later, the boy's mother could no longer live with herself and told her parents the truth: The real father was a young man in the village. The parents were astonished and went to the holy man and begged his forgiveness for what their daughter had done. When they asked if they could have the child back, the holy man simply replied, "Is that so?"

Become aware.

It's a good practice to watch life as
you would a movie: Be completely
involved with it while it's happening,
and then leave it behind when it's
done. This is the way of detachment.

Feel gratitude
for everything.

When we see every situation
as being perfect just the way it is,
happiness grows and grows.

Two frogs were happily hopping around

when they saw a big pail sitting in front of them. They both were so interested that they couldn't control themselves—they decided to jump up onto the rocks around them to see if they could find out what was inside the bucket. When they couldn't see from that vantage point, they decided to jump in together, splashing into a pail of cream.

At first they were thrilled and drank until they could drink no longer . . . and then they realized that they couldn't get out. Each time they jumped, they hit up against the slippery side of the bucket and fell back in. They kept trying and trying, until the bigger one said, "I can do this no longer. I'm too tired." He gave up and drowned in the bucket.

The little frog told himself, *I'd rather die trying to get out of here than just give up and sink to the bottom.* He continued to paddle and paddle and then he'd try to jump, only to hit the side and slip down again. This went on for some time, until as he was paddling he felt something solid under his foot. He stepped on to this solid thing, jumped, and he was out of the bucket! By continuing to paddle, he'd churned the cream into butter, and was able to jump out.

Never give up, for we never know when the moment when everything will change will come.

Be thankful for anyone in your life who's a problem.

They're your teachers, for they show
you where you truly stand. A great saint once
said to a disciple who came to him complaining
about someone else: "He is your greatest blessing.
In fact, if he were not here, it would behoove
us to go out and find one like him."

Be
watchful
of those
who bring
only praise.

Not because what they say isn't true,
but rather because you might start believing
their words and begin acting differently.

I was once in the temple of a very great saint,

and while I was there I watched his people physically beat up someone who didn't follow their directions. I was appalled and went over to try to stop it. They looked at me with such hatred and contempt, as if to say, "Do you want some of this, too?" It troubled me so much that I spoke to a friend of mine at the temple and asked his help in understanding how something like this could happen there. He said that he had no idea and suggested that I ask the teacher. So the next day, as I was heading up for a blessing, I decided I would.

En route, I reconsidered, thinking, *This is my third day here . . . this man could be my teacher, so maybe I shouldn't question his teachings on such short notice.* I resolved that if I didn't understand it better in a week's time, I'd ask him then. As I stepped up for the blessing, he looked at me and asked what my question was. I told him I had no question. He looked right through me and said, "If you don't have a question for me, then I have one for you: Why when you look around this place all you see is power trips, and when I look around this place, all I see is love? Please answer that for me." I returned to my place totally changed.

Watch the grass grow.

No matter how many people tread upon it, no matter how many storms strike away at it, it continues to grow upward. That is your true nature. Nothing or no one can stop you from doing what is yours to do.

Fear debilitates.

When we're scared, we stand like a deer caught in the headlights: not able to move away from the very thing that frightens us. To escape fear, all we have to do is keep moving.

Create space in your mind.

Whenever you find yourself thinking that you're right, step back and allow your mind to expand. For the moment, assume that others understand why you believe what you believe and still choose to believe differently. And see if you can truly understand why they believe the way they do.

When I was in the yeshiva (a Jewish seminary), we'd spend hours, sometimes days, trying to understand a particular interpretation of a teaching. As soon as we thought we understood it, we'd find a teacher who saw it differently. We did what I suggested above and went back and forth between the two interpretations for months trying to really understand why each side believed the way they did. What a great practice for allowing us to see other points of view, for how do we ever know that we're right? A belief is not a fact; it is simply what we believe.

Create space in your heart.

When the pain of life fills you completely, open your heart a little more. Pain tries to close the heart, and fear locks it closed. When you open up, fear can't fill you, for there are no walls to hold it.

Create space in your soul.

Meditate on the thought that there are many ways to get home, and everyone has their own route. When you find your soul shutting out other possibilities, create space to allow for another way.

*Live life
in the present.*

This moment is the
only thing that's real.
Worrying about the future
and lamenting the past only
crowds out the beauty of
what is happening now.

Be yourself.

People will try to change
you into what they
think you should be.
When they're right, listen;
when they're not, have the
courage to be yourself.

A certain teacher,

known for the simplicity of his ways, came to the village where a very learned scholar had a large following. The students of the learned man left their teacher to go see this simple wandering man. While in his presence, they were struck by the love that flowed from him and were swept away by the love that he cultivated in their own hearts.

Seeing the effect this man was having on his students, the learned scholar went out to teach him a lesson. He asked questions that were meant to trick him with the complexity of the knowledge required to answer. The simple man simply replied, "All that is necessary is that you love completely." The scholar tried again to ask another question, and the simple man again stated, "All that is necessary is that you love completely." The scholar was getting frustrated, yet he couldn't help feeling a love in his heart that he'd never felt before.

At that moment, the simple man asked the scholar to come up to him. As he came forward, the simple man touched him on the forehead, and the scholar tumbled to the ground with what seemed like convulsions. When he finally stood up, he said with tears in his eyes, "For years I've studied and studied the teachings, and in one moment, I understand more about them than I have in all those years. How is that possible?"

The simple teacher looked at him and just said, "All that is necessary is that you love completely."

A wise person once said,

"Be center everywhere, circumference nowhere." That is, when we live from our center, we embrace all beings as our own.

The other day, someone told me,

"I'm afraid that if I do that, I'll lose the core of my being." The core of our being is who we are—how could we ever lose that? No one and no thing can ever take our core away from us.

Two frogs lived together in a pond.

Day and night, they swam together and were content with the life they had. One day the little frog jumped onto the land and told his friend that he was going to explore what was around them. Soon he was on the top of a hill and couldn't believe his eyes: On one side he spied the little pond he'd known his whole life, but on the other side, there was water as far as his eyes could see. Clearly, this was the biggest lake he'd ever seen!

Excitedly, he hopped down to his friend, told him what he'd seen, and beckoned him to come with him. His friend didn't believe him and couldn't be convinced to leave the small pond, asking the little frog what could be bigger than what they already had. After trying his best to talk his friend into coming with him, the little frog hopped off and lived forever in the wonderful big lake he saw.

So often we think that where we are is all that exists, when right over the horizon is something so much greater than we could ever imagine. We simply need to be willing to take the risk to go somewhere we haven't been and do something we haven't done.

Fear not the punishment of some vengeful god—

the punishment we strike upon ourselves is far more damaging.

Why not love ourselves exactly as we are?

We don't need to lose weight or grow hair or change anything, for once we do so, we'll find other flaws in ourselves to criticize. The pain we experience from not being at peace with ourselves exactly as we are in this moment is what we must surrender.

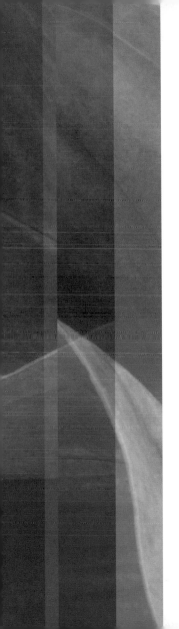

We need
to let go
of everything

that no longer serves us.
How long must we carry the burden
of the mistakes of our past?

Mentally
give away
everything

that you think belongs to you,
so if one day it were no longer there,
it wouldn't cause you a moment of suffering.

A man who had suffered much in his life

finally found his way to a monastery and asked the priest there, "I want to devote my life to the study of Zen, but I have never had the capacity to stick with anything for a long time. Is there a quick way to enlightenment?"

The teacher told him that he'd be accepted into the monastery for two days, during which he'd be taught the quick way to enlightenment. He then asked the man if there was anything he enjoyed. The man said that he wasn't good at anything because his inability to stick to things had prevented him from becoming good at anything, but he did like to play chess.

The teacher brought in a young disciple who was very learned at chess and sat the men down at a table. He took out a sword and told them that they'd play until one had beaten the other—and whoever lost the game would lose his head. Neither man could believe what he'd just heard! Since the chessboard became their life, they concentrated as never before on every move they made. At first the young disciple made moves that gave him an advantage, but then he made one big mistake.

The man seized the moment, and in that instant, the game changed in his favor. Now the young disciple was literally fighting for his life. The man had the advantage and clearly saw the moves needed to win. He looked over at the boy and saw the dedication and devotion he'd lived his life with . . . and then he thought about his own life. He realized that if someone should die, it should be himself, so he made a move that he knew would cost him the game. In that moment, the young disciple was able to take the advantage back.

The teacher, who was watching everything, walked up to the board and threw it and the pieces onto the ground. "There is no winner or loser here," he told the man. "The game is over. No heads will fall. There are only two things needed to find enlightenment: concentration and compassion. Today you learned them both. Stay with me and study the way you've played chess today, and enlightenment will be yours quickly."

Love quietly.

Practice this whenever possible: Simply send love from
your heart to the heart of another person, without
ever letting them know that you're doing so.

Love from afar.

Send love in waves to someone you barely know.
Feel that you're bathing their spirit with
the warmth of your heart.

You are so lovable!

Know that you're so easy to love.
With all your inadequacies, you're still lovable—
nothing will ever change that!

Fill your days with beautiful moments.

Every moment in and of itself is beautiful.
Throughout the day, as often as you like,
be with each moment as it
comes and goes and see
how extraordinary life
can truly be.

A man traveling from town to town

came to a field where he encountered a tiger. He turned and ran as fast as he could, only to find the tiger giving chase. As he reached a precipice, he grabbed hold of a vine and jumped. As he looked down, he saw another tiger who was looking up from below wanting to eat him. The only thing the man could do was hold on to the vine.

At that moment, he noticed two mice chewing away at the vine that held him between life and death. The man looked to his right and saw a luscious strawberry. He reached over and picked it. It tasted so good. . . .

Live life fully.

You could die at any moment,
so let no dream go unfulfilled.

Be simple.

Enjoy the simplicity of things.
Life gets complicated enough on its own.

Add nothing to life,
subtract nothing from life . . .

but live it just as it is.

The teacher gathered his students together

one evening and said, "I won't be long here in this world. My days are coming to an end, and I wanted to tell you all how proud I am of the effort you've given in your search to find enlightenment. With zeal, many of you have pursued the way, often in sacrifice of your own self—yet none of you have found what you seek. It is now time to slow down and realize that all that you seek, you already are. There is nowhere else to run, nothing else to find." Saying this, his eyes lifted and his body fell to the ground. He was gone.

Watch a mother with her baby—

and care for the world with the totality of that love.

Watch the river . . .

the way it flows and effortlessly passes over the little impediments that get in its way. That is the way to walk through life, unencumbered by the small challenges that happen every day.

Watch yourself.

What do you really like or dislike? What makes you happy or sad? Be in each moment and feel the beauty of knowing who you are.

When you take off your shoes,

leave all the problems of the world there on the floor with them. Have no fear, they'll return to you when you put your shoes back on.

The more you think about something, the more you'll crave it.

The less you think about it, the less you'll desire it. Your thoughts are your tour guides, taking you with them wherever they go.

The bamboo rod

is strong
on the
outside
and
hollow
on the
inside.
The Zen way
is to be
strong
on the
inside
and
gentle
on the
outside.

In one life
Buddha chose to be a deer,

and he became the leader of a large herd. The king at the time was a hunter, and his subjects thought to trap some beasts in a canyon so that the king could come there to hunt. They arranged an elaborate trap and then chased two herds of deer from different directions into it. It worked flawlessly, and in a very short time thousands of deer were trapped. When the king came, he saw the majesty of the two leaders of the herds and told his subjects that they weren't to be sacrificed. Nevertheless, the "Buddha deer" chose to be the first one sacrificed. Seeing this, the subjects of the king went to tell him that one of the leaders was volunteering to be sacrificed to save the others from being killed on that day.

The king came and spoke with the Buddha deer, saying that his life was spared. But the deer would hear nothing of it, for how could he serve his herd if he could let them die so that he could live? The king agreed to set his herd free, but the Buddha deer replied, "My gracious king, I cannot walk away and allow my herd to go free, for that means that I will be the cause of suffering for all the deer of the other herd."

After much deliberation and many rounds of the Buddha deer sacrificing himself so that no other creatures would suffer, the king ended up banning all hunting of wildlife in his kingdom. He ended up building a statue of the deer on the site of this conversation to remind all that we cannot live in happiness as long as others suffer.

See the world through the eyes of compassion.

Forgive everyone, embrace all,
and allow others to be exactly who they are.
You can't change them anyway.

Treat yourself with compassion.

Nothing in the world is without blemish,
so be gentle and kind to yourself
when you stumble.

At a certain monastery,

the monks noticed that one of the brothers was stealing from the others. As everyone had so little already, they went to the head of the temple and told him of the incident. The abbot said that he'd handle it and sent them off. The next day, it happened again. This time, the abbot told his monks, "Look what this brother has done to your hearts. He's stolen from you because he doesn't know the difference between right and wrong. But you, my monks, the ones who have cleansed and purified yourselves all these years, come to me with hearts full of anger at the injustice you've witnessed. If he weren't here, we would have to look for him and beg him to be a part of this monastery, for he's uncovered something in you that has long been hidden. Go now and release your anger into the acceptance of all beings."

The morning glory

opens with the light and closes with the dark,
but the Zen Mind opens to everything.

Observe the sun.

It doesn't rush to rise or hesitate to set, and it can't change a
second of its cycle. Everything in life has its time and place.
Follow the pace of nature: never rushed and never late.

See the beauty of the leaves

changing color in the fall, and the gentleness with which the
rose drops its petals. The natural course of life is to transition
with dignity and beauty. Live life so that when *you* transition,
all that remains is your integrity.

Summer, fall, winter, spring . . .

the seasons change, it's the way of life.
Everything changes, so when we hold on to what was,
we feel loss, for nothing can ever be what it once was.

Every season is beautiful—

no one is more special than another.
So too are the seasons of our life.
Each one is rich with beauty.

Relax.

Everything will resolve itself in time—
this is the way of the world. This is also the way of Zen.
Walk through life without stress or strain, and
everything will return to its place.

Lift up humanity.

Turn toward those who try to do you harm, and silently
bless them with your breath. Breathe in their pain,
and breathe out your peace.

Talk less
and less about others,

but pray more and more for them. In this way, we find
ourselves understanding, and even becoming, each other.

The evening
doesn't try to change the day,

nor does the day try to change the night. Live in this way,
never trying to change others, but rather giving them the
freedom to be as they are and seeing the beauty in them as is.

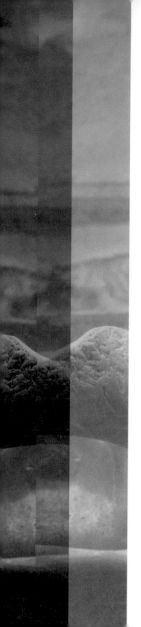

A plant
needs sunshine
and rain
in order to grow,

just as all beings need love and
suffering to grow. Therefore,
when suffering comes, drink
it in like water and allow it to
make you more beautiful.

A criminal,
well-known for his savagery,

came to the young monk and demanded that he teach him about heaven and hell. The young monk replied, "I will teach you nothing. You are a scoundrel, and there is nothing I could teach you because you are worthless. You are an idiot and live a life of destruction. You are no good. Get out of my sight."

The criminal could not believe that he'd been spoken to this way by such a scrawny little man. Never in his life had anyone said such things to him! His anger started to mount until he took out his sword and told the monk that he was going to torture him so severely that he'd wish he'd never lived. The monk looked him in the eye and said, "That is hell."

The criminal, now confused, couldn't believe that this little monk had almost lost his life to teach him what he'd come to learn. His heart filled with compassion for the small man, and his heart opened to him. The monk, seeing this transformation, then said, "That, my friend, is heaven."

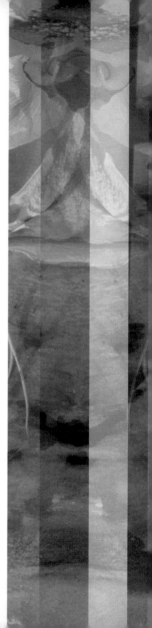

Breathe.

Your breath is the greatest tool you have to help you know exactly where you are. The quicker your breath, the more agitated you are; the deeper your breath, the more relaxed you are. Therefore, to relax in any moment, take six long, deep breaths in and out.

Be still.

The night grows still, and everyone rests. The ocean and the wind rise up and become still again; it is the way of all things to return to stillness, just as it is the way of all creation to rest.

Happiness just _is_.

It isn't something you have to earn, look for,
or wait to receive—it's always there. To find it,
simply stop looking and become it.

See the stars at night.

They seem so small to your eyes, but their light
shines for millions of miles. Be like those stars—
small in your own eyes, yet radiant to all.

The sun shines
on the rich and the poor,

the righteous and the criminal, the exalted and the
simple. When we give like the sun, our soul shines.

When the sun beams through a stained-glass window,

the colors on the floor are purple, red, green, and blue. One is not better than the other, for they're all a part of the same light. So too is humankind. Every person has a belief system that's no better or worse than any other. They're all illuminated by the same light.

Be gentle to yourself.

Know that whatever you think of yourself, you're probably ten times that in the eyes of others. Somewhere between the two is where you really are.

It's not important
what others think of you,

but it's very important what you think of yourself.

Become peace.

Bathe all you meet with your serenity.
In doing so, peace will be abundantly yours.

A friend
of mine went to practice

a certain style of meditation where he was put in a room with the door locked from the outside. Three times a day his meals were brought to him, and he had access to a restroom—otherwise, he was left alone to sit.

My friend told me that the first four hours he was there were some of the most blissful moments of his life, but as time went on, he started to wonder what was going on. Where were these people, and why hadn't they come to check on him? By the time the tenth hour rolled around, he was fuming. He was so upset that he started screaming, yet still no one came. The louder he screamed, the angrier he got; this went on for hours, and still no one came. He couldn't believe that he'd signed up for this for three days. He thought that these people were charlatans who were taking his money for nothing. What a fool he was.

At that moment the door opened. The head monk walked in and simply asked, "How are you?" My friend started to recount his angry feelings, and the monk just listened. After a long while my friend stopped, and the monk asked if he'd been angry the whole time. My friend told him of his feelings during the first four hours, and the monk asked, "What changed? Everything in the room was the same. Why in one instant did it bring you bliss and the next moment anger?" And then the monk walked out.

When life becomes difficult,

allow yourself to feel the pain in the moment. Go with it for as long as it lasts, and then watch it dissolve away. Pleasure and pain are merely states of mind, rather than situations. Every situation is neutral.

The storms of life come and go. . . .

Earthquakes, tornadoes, and hurricanes cause destruction, and then over time, the earth heals itself. Be like the earth: Walk through the tragedies of life, and then as soon as possible, rebuild yourself.

Who knows when your final day will come?

In the course of a moment, everything you know could change. Live today the way you would if you knew it was your last one on Earth. Dance more, criticize less, love more, and never be ashamed.

Become aware of what you feel.

When you see parts of yourself that you don't like, just watch the feelings come and go without getting too caught up in what it is you're feeling. Everything passes—these emotions will, too.

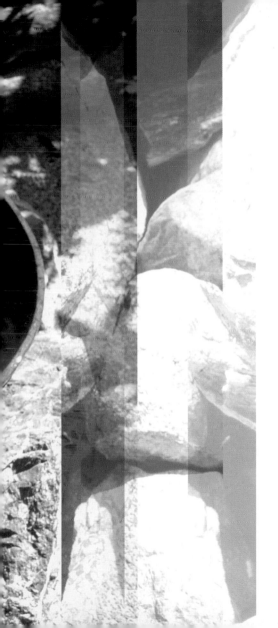

Understand the yin and the yang.

Within the white
is a dot of black,
and within the black
is a dot of white.
Nothing is ever
absolutely perfect;
therefore,
be happy
with the imperfection
of your own
being.

What is suffering?

The desire for things
to be other than they are.
What is contentment?
Accepting everything as it is.

Watch the hand on the clock move.

Second by second, time
passes—our moments on
Earth are so fleeting. Live
each moment fully and
happily, and you'll leave
joyously.

The baby eats when it's hungry,

smiles when it's happy, and cries when it's sad. This is natural. There's no second-guessing itself, no questioning what others think, no hidden agenda . . . there's simply being in the moment.

The blind man wants to see, while the seeing man is often blind.

When will we take the time to be thankful for everything we have? Why not now, before it passes us by?

Two brother monks, one wise and one simple,

had a practice of housing wandering monks if they could beat them in the debate of philosophical teachings. This particular evening, the wise monk was tired from a day of rigorous study when a wandering monk came to their door. The wise brother told the simple brother that he must dialogue with the monk in his place—but it must be done in silence. Shortly thereafter, the traveling monk returned to say that he must find lodging elsewhere because he'd lost the argument. The older brother wondered what happened.

"Well," said the traveler, "I held up one finger, representing Buddha; he held up two fingers, signifying Buddha and his teachings. I then held up three fingers representing Buddha, his teachings, and his followers living a harmonious life. He then shook his clenched fist at me, indicating that all three come from one realization. He clearly won the debate."

Shocked, the monk went to congratulate his brother on his victory when he found the young man running out the door. "Where are you going?" he requested. "I heard you won the debate."

"I won nothing," the brother stated. "I'm going to find that guy and beat him."

"Why? What happened?"

The simple brother said, "As soon as he walked in, he held up one finger, insulting me because I only have one eye. As he was a guest in our home, I thought to be polite to him, so I held up two fingers to honor the fact that he had two eyes. Then he held up three fingers to say that between us we have only three eyes. So I got mad and got up to punch him, but he went running out, and that was it."

As you can see, everything in life is colored by our perception.

From the sky, everything looks small,

but from the ground, everything looks big.
In all of life, nothing is fixed—everything
depends on perspective.

The love for a child is the greatest love of all.

Even though it's instinctual, I always wondered if
I'd love my daughter as much as I do now if she were born
to my next-door neighbor. . . . Love each other as if
we were all each other's children.

Music has the power to transcend time and space.

When we hear a song from a certain time in our lives, we're immediately taken back to those memories. That is the power of association. I remember once washing mushrooms while, at the same time, repeating a chant that had really inspired me. I felt so uplifted in those moments that every time I washed mushrooms after that, I felt inspired. Create strong associations that take you wherever you want to go.

Water flows, earth remains, fire ignites, air circulates . . .

is one more right than another? There isn't one way to live. Each being finds that which is right for them.

Be like the wind:

Blow over everything without becoming any of it.

Each week, fast for one day.

Not only from food, but also from worry, criticism, fear, and self-doubt. You'll feel rejuvenated!

Watch the seconds
tick away—

they never move backward.
We're the same: There is no backward movement.
Even if it appears to be otherwise,
we're always moving forward.

The past is over—

there are no more plans you can make for it.
The future is unknown—plan for it and
undoubtedly your plans will change.
This moment is all that exists.
Why plan for it when you can live it?

A couple sat with a doctor

as he talked to them from the heart. The woman was dying of cancer, and the doctor told her, "You are my hero. Everything I've ever learned pales at this moment when I look at you."

The woman couldn't believe her ears. He was considered to be the finest doctor in the world—people came from all over to seek his advice, and he'd literally saved thousands of lives. How was what he was telling her possible? She'd done very little in her life that had meaning to others. She was shy and reserved, and only her closest friends really knew how big her heart was.

The doctor saw the look of disbelief on her face and continued. "It's true, you *are* my hero," he said. "You're my teacher. For you live your life knowing that your days are numbered, yet you live each moment fully alive. My days are numbered, too, yet I don't really believe that they are. Because I'm healthy, I think that I'll be around forever, but I could get in a head-on collision on the way home today and die instantly. My time here on Earth could be much shorter than yours, but you live alive and I don't. Thank you for showing me how I want to live."

We all try so hard to be better people.

Better than what?
What could be better
than simply being ourselves?

The deaf person strains to hear,

while the hearing person craves silence.
Each one wants what they don't have.
Find what you want in what you
have and happiness will be assured.

In the oracle known as the I Ching,

one saying that comes up often for me is:
"It furthers one to cross the great river." In other words,
we must move forward to meet our challenges. If we hesitate,
or move before the moment is right, we lose. But if the
moment comes and we act, we will prosper.

Watch the leaves in autumn.

They change colors and then fall off the tree. Live life in
this same way. As time progresses, become more and
more beautiful, and then gently slip away.

Money, fame, and fortune

may further us in our time here, but what of it
will remain at the end of our days? Find what will remain.

Be compassionate.

Be a messenger that delivers compassion to everyone—
not through some esoteric practice, but through the
kindness of your eyes.

Breathe. Breathe again.

Breathe in acceptance, breathe out criticism. Breathe.
Breathe again. Breathe in love, breathe out hatred. Breathe
Breathe again. Breathe in whatever you want, and breathe
out whatever no longer serves you.

Watch as others battle for fame and recognition.

Let them have their glory—how long will their happiness last? Be silent and go unrecognized. Find your peace in the silence of knowing what you've truly accomplished. Pray for all sentient beings that the joy they seek be truly theirs.

It is not in the recognition of humankind

that your peace will come, but rather in the recognition of your own eyes.

Life is full of changes—

what we have today may not be what we have tomorrow.
Live each moment in gratitude for all that is.

I remember hitchhiking around the world years ago.

Somewhere along the way I met a guy who was sitting on the road, and we started to talk. When a car came by, I put out my thumb, but he just sat there. Although he'd been there for a while, he suggested that I go about 20 feet in front of him in order to get a ride. I decided to stay and find out more about this fellow.

He told me that it was easy to get a ride—what was difficult was to be able sit with yourself. "If you can sit with yourself," he said, "you never need to go anywhere. Sit and wait, if you can, for that is where the true benefit in life is." He went on to

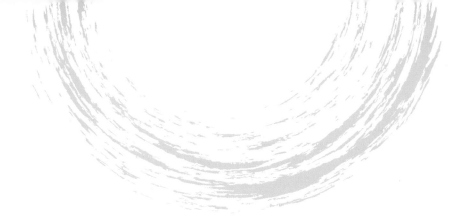

say that on occasion, people had even woken him from a deep sleep to ask if he needed a ride. "The ride that is meant for you will always come."

Astonished, I asked, "When it comes, does something significant happen?"

And he smiled and said, "Of course—you get closer to where you're going! Nothing more, nothing less. Sometimes there's conversation, sometimes not, but it always takes you somewhere."

Something about this fellow has stayed with me all these years. There was a Zen-like simplicity to his way of life, and a beauty to the way he lived without strain in this world.

Honor all that is,

and respect others' beliefs.
In this way, you'll bring an end to suffering.

*Believe in the beauty
of your own soul.*

Just as you breathe without trying to control
the inhalation and the exhalation, allow the
inner wisdom of your spirit to guide you
without the need to be in control.

What can we really control

except our ability to give up the need to control?

Make everything your meditation.

Why only sit for an hour or two a day?
Instead, let the day become a moving meditation,
and make every moment wholly conscious.

A skeptic challenged the teacher

while he was instructing a large crowd of people by saying, "Brother, they say that because of your supreme understanding, you can predict the future and know the fate of all sentient beings. Is that so?" When the teacher didn't answer, the man pushed forward, insisting, "If you're truly so wise, please answer for me the following question: Is the bird in my hand alive or dead?"

Unbeknownst to the teacher, the man held the bird in such a way that if the teacher said he was alive, which he indeed was, the man could easily squeeze the bird and kill him. And if the teacher said the bird was dead, he would simply open his hand and let the bird go.

The teacher simply replied, "The fate of that bird, my friend, is in your hand, just as the fate of your life in is your hands. Open your hand and let the bird live, and open your heart and let *yourself* live."

Take risks.

Tomorrow
you may not be able
to do what you
could do today.

Forget fear—

after all,
it will remind
you of itself enough
without your having
to think about it.

The king was very distraught

because he'd just lost his daughter. No one in the land could do anything to help him, so a wise monk was summoned. The monk counseled the king by telling him that all was perfect and just as it should be. The king was enraged by this comment and said, "If all is perfect, give me your hand!" After he cut off the monk's thumb, he barked, "Now what do you say?!" The monk repeated that all was perfect and exactly as it needed to be.

Some days later the king asked the monk to go hunting with him. While they were gone, savages from the forest surrounded them and said that they were going to take the monk to be sacrificed to their gods. The sacrifice was all set, and then they noticed that the monk didn't have a thumb. Since the savages could only sacrifice pure beings to their gods, the monk just wouldn't do.

Upon returning to the town, the king asked the monk if he still believed that everything was perfect and just as it should be. The monk answered, "I do. After all, since I had no thumb, the savages couldn't sacrifice me, so I'm here today with you."

Be peace.

Allow every situation to take you deeper into
your own sense of inner serenity.

What is good?
What is bad?

Nothing inherently is one or the other. In every situation,
good and bad could change. Therefore, see goodness in all
things until you're forced to see that they're bad.

Who are you?

Have you ever really asked yourself this simple question?
Are you the body that you wear? The job that you have?
The family you've created? The knowledge you've acquired?
The friends you've made? *Who are you?*

Live free
of the things around you.

Each evening give everything that you are back to Spirit.
Strip yourself down to that which cannot be given away,
then you'll know who you are.

Just as when we're thirsty
we drink and when we're
hungry we eat,

when we want to change, we change.
Nothing can be forced upon us, even by ourselves.

Night is dark, and day is light—

we don't expect one to become the other. Accept the natural differences that exist in life.

The bee comes to the flower for honey,

and the flower happily gives what it has without question. Live in this way: Ask for what you need, and give what you have when asked to help.

See the way of nature.

Everything coexists beautifully. The ocean adds to the beauty of the sunset, the trees give color to the mountains—nothing competes against anything else. When we live in this way, all beings prosper.

That which can be named or told is not real.

What is real is beyond name and the stories we tell about it.

Beauty and ugliness make each other exist—

without one, the other is void. When we see the beauty in duality, we become one with ourselves and everything around us.

Work without working,
and play without playing.

Do without doing, and be without being.
To live an effortless life, simply be yourself.

A wise man once said

that the whole of life comes from closing down all accounts
and not opening up any new ones. Desire nothing.
Collect no treasures that you wouldn't give away
in a moment, and peace will fill you.

Do nothing,

and all will be well.

An empty vessel is beautiful because it's empty.

Fill it and you can no longer see the vessel, but rather its functionality. Become empty and you'll see your own beauty, not merely your functionality.

The disciple planted a seed in his garden

on the day he entered into his teaching. He wished to use the growth of this flower as a symbol for his own growth along the path—he told his teacher this and invited him to come when the flower was grown to see how beautiful it had become. The teacher agreed to do so.

Every day, the student would water the seed and pull the tiny little weeds from around it. But after a few days, when the shoot had yet to push through the soil, the student started to worry. So he dug up the seed to see what was happening. Every few days he'd dig up the seed, never allowing it a chance to grow. Seeing this, the teacher told the student, "This flower is indeed a symbol of your spiritual path: Every day you want to see progress when, in fact, all you need to do is leave everything alone and it will grow naturally."

Watch the wheel and the way it spins.

The farther you get from the center, the quicker it spins.
To find peace, return to the center.

Watch nature.

It seems to be without beginning or end, so it lasts forever.
If you allow one action to flow into another without
beginning or end, life will truly be in the moment.

Watch water flow—

there's no space it doesn't fill. Be like water,
and give to everyone and everything.

In all things,
know where to stop.

Sometimes you need to finish before
the end, while other times you must go
beyond where others go. True knowledge
is knowing when to go forward . . .
and when not to.

When we concern
ourselves with
acquiring or
losing things,

the only thing we truly get is a lack
of inner peace. Yet when we accept
what we have, contentment reigns.

Live life with an open heart.

Erase judgment from your thoughts, live with compassion, and practice understanding. Keep in mind that everyone is doing the best they possibly can and realize that if they knew better, they'd do better—therefore, be gentle. Now, practice this same gentleness with yourself. Know that you're doing the best you can in every situation and honor yourself with compassion. This simple thought will help you be less critical and more appreciative of all that is.

The
present
cannot be
caught in a vessel,

nor can it be broken by a stone. It is ever changing, ever new—for as soon as you grasp it, it disappears.

The
way of nature
is unchanging.

If you look at its shorter rhythms, it seems to change endlessly, but if you watch its longer rhythms, you'll see how constant everything remains.

Do things in a way that makes others feel that they did them.

In this way, everything will get accomplished.

The teacher was walking around the room

examining the clay pots that each of his students had made. As he looked at each one, he'd gently point out little flaws in the work and give them instruction upon how to correct it. As he walked around, he'd say, "This one has a little crack here in the glaze," "This one wasn't finished smoothly," and so on. He then came to the student who was held in high regard by all the other students, but the teacher always saw only his pride. Nevertheless, the teacher approached the student's pot and it was perfect. Everything about it was beautiful—it was truly a work of art.

The teacher took out his little stick and, tapping the pot, said, "This pot is perfect."

The student couldn't contain his pride, at which point the teacher tapped the young man's head. "But *this* pot has a big crack in it," he said. The pot was perfect, but the student was flawed by his ego.

When we forget

what we should be,
we find what we are.

Give up
becoming enlightened,

and enlightenment will become you.

If you don't trust,
you'll never be trusted.

This world is a mirror reflecting
back to you what you give to it.

126

The monastery had consisted of just men for many years,

but that all changed when a beautiful young woman came to the abbot and said that she wanted to join the monastery. Although he was hesitant, the abbot was taken with the commitment and devotion of the young woman, so he told her she could join. For months the monks noticed her and most of them were fine, but several secretly fell in love with her. One of them wrote her a letter telling her that he was madly in love with her and asked that she meet him at a certain time and place. That night as the monastery sat to meditate, the young woman stood up and said, "To the monk who wrote me that letter, if you love me as much as you profess, come forward now and show me."

Find the way that is yours,

even if it means walking where no one else has gone before. Have the courage to find your own way, regardless of what those around you say.

Follow that which cannot be followed

and search for that which cannot be found. Become what never ends and never begins—that is who you really are.

The way of the universe is to fill that which is empty

and to empty that which is full. When we're full, nothing else can enter, but when we're empty, all things can come to us.

Fierce storms don't last forever.

In fact, nothing in life will remain forever—what is today will be gone tomorrow. When we hold on to our present reality, we can assure ourselves of suffering.

Avoid that which doesn't bring happiness.

It sounds so easy, yet when we look, we find that we run after many things that bring us suffering.

What does it matter how others view us?

What matters more
is how we view ourselves.

Walk gently,

leaving tracks only where they
can make a difference. Where no
difference can be made, walk without
leaving tracks. This is how the sage
passes through life: unseen and
invisible, yet effecting
change everywhere.

Become
as a
little child,

seeing all things for the first time.

See
value
in
what
is,

usefulness in what is not.
The window is useful because of what *isn't* there.

The ruler of the kingdom

tried desperately to keep his people from practicing spiritual teachings. One day, a very charismatic teacher came to the village, and the people came out in large numbers to see him. When he spoke, they'd follow everything he said. Seeing this, the king went to where the people had gathered and challenged the teacher. He said, "You may be very charismatic, and all these people may follow what you say, but that's because they respect you. I have no respect for you, so how will you get me to follow what you say?"

The teacher looked at the king and said, "I understand. Come up here with me so that the people can see their king." The king ascended to the podium where the teacher sat, and the teacher told him, "Come and sit beside me." As the king was about to sit, the teacher said, "Sit on this side so that the people will be able to see you better." The king did. The teacher then explained, "You just followed what I suggested three times. Now sit and listen so that together we can end the suffering that exists here and replace it with happiness." From that day on, the king was a disciple of the teacher.

Do you think you can change the world?

Think how difficult it is to change one thing in yourself. . . . When you let the world change itself, all things return to balance.

Things are sacred just as they are—

therefore,
change nothing
and accept everything.

A weak person uses force to rule, while a powerful person uses love to guide.

Force will one day disappear, but love will always remain.

A scorpion
was trapped on a branch

as the river started to surge. Within minutes, he'd be swept away by the current. Suddenly he spotted a frog and called out, "Save me, please save me!"

The frog looked at the scorpion and asked, "If I save you, will you promise me that you won't sting and kill me?"

"I promise," said the scorpion.

So the frog swam over and rescued the scorpion, and just as he was about to place the creature on the other side of the river, he felt a sting on his leg. He looked at the scorpion and asked, "How could you sting me when just minutes ago you promised that you wouldn't?"

The scorpion replied, "I'm a scorpion—it's my nature to sting."

Never ask someone to go against their nature. It will always sting you.

Rejoice
not in victory nor in defeat,

but rather in that which gives dignity to all.
The wise man uses weapons only when he must,
and mourns his victory in sorrow.

All things
are happy when they are still.

When we fight in order to accomplish,
we disturb the gentle balance that exists.
Therefore, the wise man never fights but remains still.

When we know others,
we become wise;

when we know ourselves, we become enlightened.

The one who has the courage to let things remain as they are

is the one who sees that he's not in control. He offers his power back to the universe and becomes strengthened by it.

Face fear straight on.

For years I ran and hid from it, shivering in the corner and hoping that I'd never have to face it. One day I grew tired of being scared, so I opened the door that hid me from my fear, only to find it was no longer there. *I* was the one who had kept myself bound for all that time.

There are so few real people:

those who love for the sheer joy of loving, people who give
to ensure that others succeed. What pleasure is found
in helping others get what they want!

All beings want to be
loved and accepted,

and we have it within our power
to give them what they want.

Greatness flows everywhere.

Pride flows nowhere.

Meditate
not because you'll
feel holy,

but so you'll know that there's no
difference between the times that
you sit and the times you don't.

Everything
returns to what
remains.

Run after it, and you'll find it;
sit patiently, and it will find you.

Succeed quietly,

letting everyone else believe
that it was because of their efforts
that a venture worked.
At times, you may feel
unrewarded for your efforts,
but you'll always know
in your heart the value
of your contributions.

That which cannot be seen
or heard can never
be exhausted.

Therefore, restore yourself
with what cannot be seen or heard.

When we accept
people exactly as they are,

we have true peace.

It doesn't matter what happens to us,

but rather what we become in the process.
It's not the things in our life that need to change, it's us.

That which is big now will one day be small,

while that which is small today will grow tomorrow.
So relish not in what passes but rather in what remains.

A student came to his teacher to learn Zen.

Before the lesson, the teacher poured tea into the student's cup, continuing to pour until tea was flowing onto the floor. Finally, the student asked why he continued to pour when the cup was obviously full. The teacher smiled and said, "You come to me like that cup, full of your own self. When you empty your cup, come back to learn Zen."

After sitting in meditation under the bodhi tree,

Buddha got up and started
walking to the marketplace.
His first disciples looked at him
and said, "I want to walk like that."
So, Buddha's first sermon had no words;
but rather, people saw something in him
that they wanted, and they followed him.

Buddha always said,

"You could search the world far and wide to find someone more deserving of your love and affection than yourself, but you'll never find that person. You yourself are more deserving of that love than anyone in the universe."

As a child, Buddha saw the farmer planting seeds into the ground.

While others rejoiced at the planting of food, Buddha saw the turmoil that the plow forging into the earth caused with the creatures of the soil. Even as a child, he saw the suffering of beings: In the wholesome act of planting food, lives were still being destroyed. And it set in motion his lifetime goal to end suffering in all beings.

As an exercise today, try to become aware of the suffering we cause without even realizing it.

When we're truly ourselves,

we're awake among sleeping people. The energy that radiates from us awakens others. The words we say mean nothing— it's our energy that transforms.

Not long ago
I spoke to a woman who said

that she longed so much to meditate, yet she couldn't calm her mind. I said, "Fine. Instead of calming your mind, just watch it. As your thoughts wander, wander with them. Watch them go from place to place and see what happens." Several days later she told me that as soon as she stopped trying to control her mind, it stopped battling her and just relaxed on its own. Funny how that works, isn't it?

It's said that when the student is ready, the teacher will come.

A friend of mine was often curious to know if this would be true in terms of finding a relationship. He wondered how it would be possible for the woman of his dreams to just come knocking on his door. And then, through an Internet dating service, the woman of his dreams not only knocked on his door, but came right into his living room.

A friend was telling me of a problem

she was having with another—each time she talked to this person, he cut her down. We give others the power to make us feel bad. Why? No one has that power unless we give it to them. Instead of choosing not to see the people who annoy us, why not visit them more often and continue to be the person we are, no matter what they choose to do. They have the right to be whoever they want to be, just as we do.

Practice being yourself everywhere.

A very successful emergency-room doctor

was swimming with his daughter in the ocean, when she was suddenly bitten by a dangerous fish. Blood gushed from her foot, and the doctor became very distraught. As it turned out, his daughter was fine—but in the aftermath, the father lamented the fact that he wasn't able to be that emergency-room doctor. After all, dealing with emergencies was how he made his living! Yet when it was his own flesh and blood, all his experience left him, and he was just a dad worried about his child. How could he treat her like every other person in the world? Such is the power of attachment.

This story hits me hard every time I read it, for I know how attached I am to my daughter, and I don't think it's right *not* to be so. Yet I know that one day I must give up that attachment, too, and see the whole world as my daughter. . . .

When things outside of us make us happy,

we can then assume that if we lose these things, so too goes our happiness. When we're happy with everything just the way it is, no one or no thing can take our happiness from us.

When no one is doing what you think is right,

do it yourself.

The teacher went to see a holy man

who had left this worldliness of life behind to enter seclusion in a cave to find perfect peace. The teacher traveled far up the mountain to find this man, and when he did, the holy man wasn't happy to be found.

Immediately, the teacher started to talk to him, and the holy man, who had been in silence for the past 20 years, was startled. "What is it you want?" he asked.

"I want to know why you've come all the way up here," the teacher inquired.

With a slight look of pride on his face, the holy man said, "I came here to find perfect peace."

"How foolish!" the teacher laughed. "Men like us can never find that."

The holy man rose, stared at his visitor, and bellowed, "How dare you come and disturb my meditation with this?! Get out of here this instant!"

The teacher stood up and looked him in the eye. "Where is the perfect peace you sought now?" he asked. "Come down the hill with me, and I'll teach you how to have what you seek."

The holy man left his mountaintop, and on the walk down to the village, became enlightened.

Ask 1,000 people what Zen is,

and you may receive 1,001 different answers.

There's a famous saying in Buddhism:

"If you see the Buddha on the road, kill him." I have always understood it to mean that when we find ourselves acting holy, we must kill the "holy man" and just be ourselves. But I see it another way, too: See the Buddha everywhere. Treat everyone and everything as if they were the Buddha. Kill the thought that he is a man who lived long ago, and see him in every single thing.

Two dogs walk into a room.

One comes out
quivering, barking in
fear the whole time,
while the other comes
out wagging his tail,
with a seemingly big
smile across his face.
A man seeing this
walks into the room to
discover that it's full
of mirrors. That is the
way of this life: What
we see is who we are.

A story is told of two monks who had taken a vow to never touch a woman.

They're on pilgrimage to a holy temple when they come to a place where the water has risen, making it difficult to pass. Stranded along the bank is a beautiful young lady who asks for their help. The first monk scowls at her and says that he's taken a vow of chastity, so he cannot help her. The second picks the woman up and carries her silently across the water. A mile later, the first monk asks the second, "What did you do? You know that we're not allowed to touch women—why did you take her across the river?"

The second monk answers, "Brother, I picked her up, carried her across the river, and set her down. You've been carrying her for the past mile."

Why do we think that it's only the things that we do that matter and not the things we think?

A famous storyteller came to a town,

and a big group of people gathered around him. He had to shout his story so that everyone could hear. After the crowd had dissipated, he was still shouting. Someone asked why he was yelling when there was nobody there to listen.

The sage said, "In the beginning I had to scream so that others could hear my story, but now I must scream so that *I* can hear the story."

So often, we teach what we most need to learn.

A student came to his teacher

after many years of studying mindfulness. The teacher asked him when he came into this house and took off his shoes, did he place them to the left or right of the umbrella? The student didn't know and went away to study more before coming back to his teacher.

Mindfulness comes in the everydayness of life, not only in what we think is sacred.

A friend of mine went to visit a great teacher

and while he was there, the disciples wanted him to convert to the ways of this teacher. My friend already had a teacher and he was perplexed by the dogmatism of these young disciples. When he met the teacher, he asked why his students were so dogmatic. The teacher responded, "Isn't it a little dogmatic of you to think that they're dogmatic?"

When you walk, walk; when you eat, eat; and when you sit, sit.

This is the way of Zen.
Do what you do fully in each moment.

There is a very popular saying in the East:

"Trust in God, but tie your camel."

Often,
in our quest to be spiritual

we miss the messages that come to us every day. For example, on a man's first date with a woman, he gave her a rose. They enjoyed each other immensely during the next month, they were attracted to each other, and they had many things in common . . . but they didn't follow the same teacher. The woman called him to say that she couldn't see him again as she didn't want to get serious with someone of another faith. She signed off by saying, "I wanted to tell you that something weird happened. The rose you gave me a month ago still looks and smells as fresh as it did the day you gave it to me."

The love these two felt for each other was obvious, but their faith got in the way of them getting to know each other better. You see, miracles don't matter when beliefs are frozen—nothing can change them.

The bird got so used to being in its cage

that even when the door was left open, it didn't fly out. I marvel at how many times I've stayed where I am, "uncomfortably comfortable," rather than take a risk to become new again. This is the opposite of the Zen Mind, which is always new, always fresh, and always alive.

Brother Lawrence,

a simple Christian saint, was out walking when he noticed a tree losing its leaves. This act, which he'd seen probably thousands of time before, sent him into a state of enlightenment. This is the Zen Mind: suddenly seeing something again for the first time.

During the Indian-Pakistani war,

a bus got caught in a hole caused by one of the many bombs. The driver of the bus asked the passengers to get out and push to get them out. After ten minutes, the bus hadn't budged an inch, so the driver got off to try to figure out why. Imagine his surprise when he saw half the passengers at the front of the bus pushing backward and the other half at the back pushing forward! This is what we do all the time with our energy. The Zen Mind guides without resistance, harnessing all energies in one direction.

A temple priest

was getting ready for the sacred ceremony he was about to
perform. The people started gathering early because he'd
come such a long way to participate on this day. As the
ceremony was about to begin, a stray dog wandered close
to the altar. Without much ado, the priest took the dog by
the collar and tied him to a nearby tree—then he began the
ceremony. Years later, no one could remember what the priest
said, but they did remember that before the ceremony could
start, they had to tie a dog to a tree. Tying a dog to a tree
became the ceremony.

Be mindful of meaningless actions that we give great
merit to. Conversely, anything done with devotion is sacred.

When I was studying in the yeshiva,

there were so many times that I'd ask the Rabbi why things were the way they were. I was always so let down because the great teachers never seemed to be able to live up to what they themselves taught. I remember him looking me squarely in the eye and saying, "Where there is no man, *you* be the man." In other words, do what no one else has done. Don't use the fact that they haven't succeeded to lower your dream. Dream *your* dream, and then become it.

That
same
Rabbi
would
tell
me,

"Danny, when you die and meet your maker, he's not going to ask why you weren't Moses the great teacher. Instead, he'll wonder why you weren't yourself."

Seven blind men approach an elephant.

When asked to describe what the animal is, each comes up with an entirely different answer. The one holding the trunk describes the elephant as a very flexible tubelike structure, but the one holding the leg disagrees and says that it's like a pillar, strong and immovable. This goes on, with each man disagreeing with the others—yet at the same time, they're perfectly describing their personal experience of the elephant. They're each right and wrong at the same time. Often we're like these blind men: sure that our experience is right when it's just a piece of the entire puzzle. It's so important not to lose sight of the forest through the trees.

A teacher moved into town,

and after being there for some time, he still had no furniture. When asked why his house was so sparse, he replied, "My house is in heaven—why glorify this temporary dwelling?" While I understand the beauty of living with that type of awareness, I'd rather create sacred spaces wherever I find myself and not wait for some time in the future, however promising it may be.

A great teacher once said:

"It is easy to believe when thousands of people follow the same beliefs, but would we have the courage to believe if we woke up tomorrow and everyone believed differently?" *This* is true belief—to believe what we do because it is *really* what we believe.

How is it that
millions of people
become artists,

but only one is a Leonardo da Vinci; millions learn music,
but only one becomes Mozart? There is an art and a science
to everything in this world. In all things, learn technique,
but also tune in to the art behind the technique,
for that is what separates "good" from "great."

I have a friend who is perhaps the most creative person I know.

In her younger years, she was artistic—an incredible poet and writer who also played a musical instrument very well. She was thinking about being an artist until someone told her that she wouldn't make money at it. And then, everything changed: She no longer wrote, painted, or played her guitar; instead, she spent all of her time trying to convince herself that she was a businesswoman. To this day, she's had some limited success in her field, but every time I talk to her, she tells me that it's so difficult for her to function in that world.

I wonder why it isn't all right to be who we are. When will we stop trying to live up to the expectations of those around us and just do well in the things we excel at?

A newly married couple was walking along the beach

when the husband noticed a thorn in the sand and picked up his beloved to carry her past it. Five years later, that same couple was walking the same stretch of beach when the husband noticed the thorn and took his wife's arm and gently walked her around it. Five years later, upon seeing the thorn, the man told his wife, "Watch out, there's a thorn over there." Five years later, the man yelled at his wife, "We've been walking this stretch of beach for years—don't you know that there's a thorn there?! Can't you remember anything?!" This is the familiar mind, which is the opposite of the Zen Mind.

While vacationing with my daughter,

I received a call from a friend asking if I was getting any time to myself to relax or if my daughter was just running me ragged. I replied that I went on a vacation to be with my daughter, not to be on my own. Being with her *was* relaxing. And I realized that when we accept what is as it is without any need to change it or "make it better," everything is restful. It's only when we think it should be other than it is that there is stress.

*When
we are
with people,
be 100 percent
with them;*

when we're by ourselves,
be 100 percent alone. This is the
way of all things: Be exactly where
we are at any given moment and
everything will be without strain.

Once a great teacher sat with his students.

One who had been suffering with a certain situation for some time asked what he should do to overcome it. The teacher answered, "Do nothing. Just sit with it a little longer." But the student couldn't wait anymore, so he left the teacher and the practice he was following, never to return.

The teacher shed a tear and said to those who remained, "Had he made it through this last test, he would have been enlightened. Had he lasted a few more moments, everything would have changed."

We can never know what's around the next corner.

When the people
of a certain town

heard that the military was headed in their direction, and the person leading the charge was a commander most known for his cruelty, everyone fled—except for one old monk. When the commander arrived, he asked the monk, "Why didn't you flee like the others? Don't you know who I am? I'm the one who can run a sword through you without batting an eye."

The old monk looked at him and replied, "My dear friend, I am the one who can have a sword run through me without batting an eye." In that moment, the commander become a disciple of the monk and never again acted with cruelty.

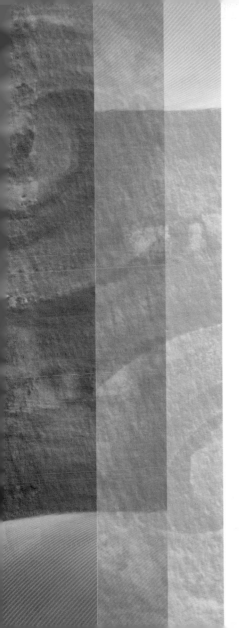

A wandering Buddhist teacher

came to a village and said that if anyone could sit with him in total concentration for 24 hours, enlightenment would be his. The people of the village thought that this didn't seem so unreasonable, so they sat with the teacher. After some time, their concentration wavered and they started again. At the end of the day, no one was enlightened, but everyone understood how difficult it was to focus their minds for even a few minutes, let alone 24 hours. It was then that the teacher was able to start teaching.

Many of us have heard the story of the man

who lost his keys outside in the dark, yet he was searching for them in the light of his house. And if you're like me, you'd wonder why someone would do that. One day I realized that I'm always looking to solve my problems with solutions that aren't the answer. No one else ever needs to change—the only thing that needs to change in order to make my life better is for me to accept life and people as they are.

I was talking to someone

the other night who told me that for ten years she's longed for intimacy with her husband, yet no matter what she's tried, she's never been able to have it. I asked her if she ever tried accepting her husband exactly the way he was rather than wanting him to be someone else. I shared with her that that's real intimacy to me. I think that it genuinely can be that simple.

While the priest of the temple was gone,

someone stole the temple incense burner. All day long, the priest focused on a certain young man who'd just joined the temple and scolded himself for not seeing it sooner. Everything about this young man cried "Thief!"

As he was cleaning the dishes that evening, the priest found the incense burner drying by the fire, freshly polished and gleaming with a beauty he'd never seen before. And that evening when he looked at the young man, he saw a beautiful disciple with a heart of gold and a soul to match.

An old wandering monk came into a village

where he'd never been. The people gathered around and waited for him to speak, but the only thing he asked was if there was a well nearby. The villagers answered that there was, and they led him to it. The monk took out his cup and handed it to a young man, asking if he could have a drink of water. The young man at the well said, "I'm unworthy to serve you, as I have no merit."

The monk replied, "I didn't ask you if you had merit, I asked if you had water."

In the beginning of life,

we're on fire and want to change the world. Yet as we get older, we realize how difficult that is, so we think that if we can have a positive influence on those around us, we'll have lived a worthwhile life. As we get older still, we understand that we can change no one, and simply look for the courage to change ourselves.

The story is told of Mara,

the God of evil, watching with his students a man discovering a piece of paper with a truth written on it. The students asked Mara, "How can you sit there with that big smile on your face? Can't you see what just happened? That man has just discovered a truth."

Mara smiled and said, "Don't worry, just watch and see. Soon he'll make a dogmatic belief out of it."

My daughter has a developmental delay.

For many years, I could not accept that her life was destined to be lived in a world of her own making, so I tried every possible thing that I could to make her life better. Yet, perhaps because she's delayed, she's more intuitive than most and often communicates through reading my thoughts and planting thoughts in my head. It happens so often now that I sometimes forget that we haven't said anything out loud.

One day she looked at me and said in her thoughts, "Daddy, why are you trying to change me so much? Is there something wrong with me the way I am? Why not just accept me for who I am and don't worry about trying to make my life better. It's great just the way it is." Just as tears were coming to my eyes, she came over and gave me a great big hug. On that day, she taught me one of the greatest lessons of my life without ever saying a word.

The student was about to become the teacher.

For years, he'd been selected as the one who would carry on the teachings of his teacher. Now the moment had finally come. The teacher brought him in and gave him a book that carried the tradition of *his* teachers, for the last several generations. It had been handed down from one teacher to the next as a rite of passage, and he was now offering the book to the student to keep safe for the next generations.

Upon receiving the book, the student threw it in the fire and said, "For years you've taught me, and never once have you shown me this book. Why do you now try to trap me with knowledge that's outside of me?" And he turned and left.

A man was passionately in love

with a woman, and every day he wrote down his love
for her. One day she arrived so that she could be with him.
He prepared himself for her, taking his ritual bath and
draping himself in the finest of garments. Finally she was
there in front of him, and he took out all his writings
to show his love for her. He went over them one by one,
until she looked at him and said, "Those are about me
and your passion for me, but now I sit in front of you.
Throw them away and enjoy the moment."

A story is told of a very beautiful woman

who wanted to join a monastery, but because of her beauty, no one would let her in. Time after time the woman was rejected and not allowed to join because she was the most beautiful woman the monks had ever seen. Deciding that she wanted this life no matter what, the woman disfigured her face by setting it on fire—no one ever looked at her again. Even though her outer beauty may have been gone, she became enlightened shortly after.

A young student asked his teacher

about the power of delusion. He said, "I don't understand how it can have such power over people, when we in the monastery are so protected." The teacher touched him on the forehead and asked if he'd get him a glass of water. . . .

While the student went to do so, he met a woman and fell madly in love with her. They got married and had two children. While they were vacationing at the beach, the strong current pulled the wife out and she screamed for help. The student, now a middle-aged man, went in after her, but his children were afraid. So he came back to take them in with him.

As he reached for his wife, the hand of one of his children slipped from his grip, and the child went down under the water. In his panic, he reached for the child with the other hand, and now his wife and other child were taken by the current. In his despair, the student closed his eyes and gave himself to the current, too. . . .

Several moments later, the teacher found the young man sleeping on the floor and awoke him by saying, "I send you for a glass of water, and I find you sleeping on the floor. *This* is the power of delusion. Never forget it."

A thief once broke into the home of a Zen master

but found nothing to steal. The master told him, "You've come all this way, and I have nothing for you—but you cannot leave empty-handed." He took off his clothes and gave them to the confused thief. After he left, the master looked at the full moon outside his window and said, "If only I could have given him the moon."

When the master was young,

he used to deliver profound lectures to his brother disciples. Some time later, his mother heard about this and wrote him to say that she didn't think he entered the monastery to become a parrot speaking words. She wished for him to stop this lecture business and find himself a cave in the mountains. She felt that in order to attain true realization, he should live out the rest of his life in silence and meditation.

The young boy
watched for years

as older men would visit the master. They'd ring the gong outside to announce their presence, bow at the door, and enter the room where the master sat. One day, the young boy decided that he too would visit the master. He rang the gong, bowed, and entered the master's room. The teacher looked at the boy and told him that he was too young to start learning. The boy wouldn't accept this, so the master said, "You know the sound of two hands clapping. Go now and return only when you can tell me the sound of one hand clapping."

The boy went away and sat for many months. When he returned, the teacher told him that he didn't have the answer. Again the boy left and sat, only to return to find the same result. This happened many times until one day the boy entered deep meditation and found the silence behind all sounds. This time, when he returned, he had indeed realized the sound of one hand clapping.

When the window was dirty, the man couldn't see through it;

when the window was clean, he couldn't see the window. The beauty of the window was that he couldn't see it. The beauty of the Zen Mind is that it causes no interference.

A pickpocket entered the village square

where the teacher
was lecturing. He walked
around looking to see who
had something he wanted. He
did not see a teacher before him or
hear the words that were changing
the lives of those gathered there. He
saw only their pockets. A pickpocket
can only see the pockets of a saint.
Similarly, we can only see what
we look for in others.

A student came to his teacher and said that he was confused.

He'd been observing his teacher give counsel now for several months, and it seemed that the teacher never gave the same advice. Not only that, he appeared to give contradictory advice to his students. The student asked for an explanation, for he could find none on his own.

The teacher answered, "It's really quite simple. It's as if I'm looking at each situation from a perch above, helping others find the center. Some are to the left, and I tell them go right; others are to the right, and I tell them to go left. To those below, I say go up; to those above, I say go down. The words are not important—finding our center is all that matters."

The master swordsman came to the monk

and told him that he finally understood that everything is one. There is no "you" or "me," but rather just emptiness that encompasses everything. The monk took out a stick and struck the swordsman over the head. The swordsman was beside himself with rage and came after the monk. At that point the monk replied, "Emptiness is quick to show anger, isn't it?"

The world is a mirror:

What we see is who we are.

A teacher
in the village
was jealous

of the crowds that another wandering monk was gathering. He went out and immediately challenged the new instructor by saying, "My teacher had such power through the practice of chanting that he could do miracles. He held a brush, and his student would hold the canvas on the other side of the river. With the flip of his wrist, he could write the Sutras on that canvas."

The wandering teacher looked at him and said, "That's wonderful, but that's not the miracle of the Zen I follow. The miracle to me is that when I'm hungry, I eat, and when I feel thirsty, I drink."

The monks gathered around Buddha

and asked him to teach them renunciation. He told them the following story: "A man who lives alone on an island realizes that the time has come to cross the water, but the water is filled with dangerous fish and there is no bridge to cross. So the man builds himself a boat made of sticks and branches, and after a difficult journey, he's able to paddle his way to the other side. Upon reaching that side, should the man keep the boat so that he can return to his island or discard it?"

The monks were divided in their response, so Buddha continued: "The man of renunciation discards the raft, knowing that he will be provided for in some other manner. The man of this world keeps the raft so that in the event that he wants to journey back, the fruits of his efforts have not gone to waste. Which are you, my monks?"

When
Buddha was asked,

"What is the totality of the Buddhist way?"
he answered, "Seeing with the eyes, hearing
with the ears, smelling with the nose, feeling
with the hands, and tasting with the mouth."

"Could that possibly be the totality of the
Buddhist way?" asked another.

To which Buddha replied, "Anything
other than this would be empty words,
for it would be outside my experience."

After having seen a man of pride,

a great teacher told one of his students, "If you ever see me acting in a manner such as that—with such pride—please do me a favor and kick me in the behind." The student looked at the teacher and asked if he really meant that. The teacher responded that of course he meant it, as he never wanted to be so full of ego.

The student, looking the teacher in the eye, said, "Bend over!"

The teacher had slipped along the path

and was being held accountable for his actions. He gathered his students around and taught them a beautiful lesson. He instructed that they should never see the part of themselves that has failed, but rather view their lives as if they just hadn't succeeded yet. He asked that they hold him in this same regard as well, saying that a slip is not a fall. But that same teacher didn't practice what he taught, for he condemned those who condemned him rather than seeing them in the way he wanted to be seen.

It's a lesson I'll never forget.

Empty yourself

of everything.

When asked one time,

"What is the highest dharma a man can offer in service of mankind?" Buddha responded, "Chopping wood and carrying water." The practice of Zen is not about lofty lectures and philosophical teachings, but rather, it's the simple awareness of everyday life.

Abandon selfishness,

desire nothing,
crave simplicity.

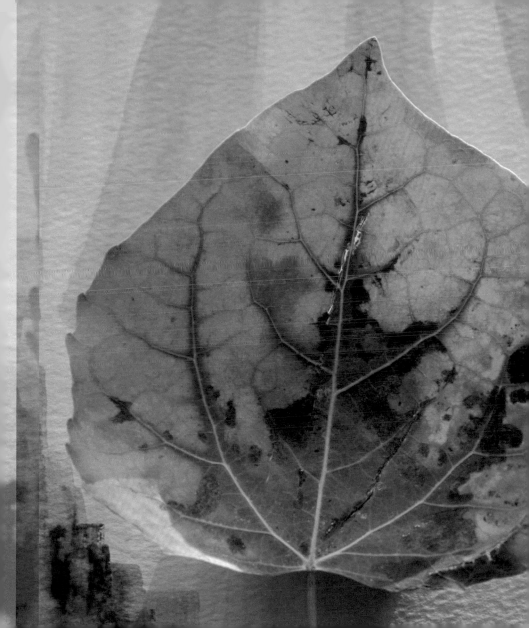

I remember being at Disneyland

many years ago with someone who was visiting there for the first time. In those days, they used to have a boat ride that ran along an obstacle course. As the boat moved, things would jump up and attack it, spray it with water, or appear to be on a collision course with it. I remember that my friend sailed the boat by taking every precaution to gets us safely across the water. When his wife asked him a question, he replied, "Not now! Can't you see how much I have to concentrate to get through this obstacle course?"

Little did he realize that the boat was on a track and nothing he did would make a difference in our passage from start to end. I always thought this to be analogous to life: We toil so hard, thinking that what we do is so important, when quite possibly we're on a track and everything in our life is already being cared for by something greater than ourselves. Wouldn't that be interesting?

A man walked into a Shiva temple

[Shiva is the Hindu God of destruction—the destroyer of bad habits and so forth]. In the middle of the room was a lingam [a phalliclike stone]. The man sat down on the floor and put his feet up on the lingam.

The priest of the temple rushed in and asked, "Don't you know what a sin you've just done? No one can put their feet on such a holy shrine! The punishment for such an act is eternity in hell."

The man, humble in his way, answered, "Please accept my apology, for I did not know that what I did was wrong. Can you please place my feet somewhere where God won't be offended?"

Immediately, the priest took the man's feet off the stone and threw them to the ground. To the man's surprise, before his feet could touch the ground, another Shiva lingam appeared to catch them. Not believing his eyes, the priest again threw the man's feet from the second lingam to the floor. And once again, a lingam appeared to catch the man's feet.

This time the humble man, with a glimmer in his eye, asked the priest to place his feet where God did not exist. At that, the priest bowed to the feet of this holy man and apologized.

The holy man replied, "There is no place where God is not."

Afterword

This book starts and ends with the same story. It is done on purpose. It is an exercise in the Zen Mind. Read it again as if you never heard it before. Allow its message to go deep within you and then return to the book's sayings and stories and read them one at a time. Sit with them for the day, week, or whatever time feels comfortable until you feel that you have gotten all that they have to give you at that moment. Some may not have much to give; others may give abundantly. May one of these sayings touch you, and may all suffering cease to exist.

Acknowledgments

I'd like to thank the following special people:

- Louise L. Hay, for creating Hay House, which is by far the best place I've ever worked. Thank you, Louise, for letting me be a part of what you have created.

- Reid Tracy, for giving me countless opportunities to succeed. Reid, you are a gem of a man, and I learn and benefit just by being around you.

- Jill Kramer and Shannon Littrell for their editorial expertise.

- I would like to thank all those who are my teachers. Some of you I have had the great privilege to sit with and learn right by your side. I learned as much watching the way you lived your life as from your words. You've taught me wisely, and I'm honored to have been able to learn from you. I would like to thank those of you who have taught me even though you had no idea you were doing so: You've been the smile for no reason, the gentle word of encouragement, the person who's been there when no one else was, and the thorn in my side who showed me where I truly stand in the cold, hard light of day and how much I still have to grow. You are my *true* teachers. I bow to each of you silently.

- My daughter, for showing me that what I most feared (having a child with some form of developmental delay) was in fact my biggest blessing. The love you've brought to me is beyond measure. Thank you, Elisa.

- And finally, to all of you who hold this book in your hands: May these words have the blessing to end suffering and bring lasting true happiness to all sentient beings.

About the Author

Daniel Levin, the author of the *Zen Cards* and the *Zen* journal, has been involved in religious studies for more than 25 years. Just one day away from being ordained as a rabbi, he left the seminary and took up the practice of yoga and meditation. For 20 years he studied and taught the principles of yoga, only to find that the time had come to leave the comfort of everything he believed behind, so he set out to find a different life.

One day, while doing nothing in particular, he heard a voice guide him to his solitary practice of Zen. Daniel belongs to no temple and follows no particular teacher, but finds his lessons in his interaction with every moment.

Daniel is also the founder and owner of ZENSei, Inc., a clothing company that offers unique and original clothing that helps people relax and feel peace. He lives in Southern California by the beach with his daughter. For more information, please visit his Website at: **www.ZENseiOnline.com**.

About the Photographer

Jerome Alfred Johnson is a freelance writer and photographer who has been a Zen practitioner since 1982. He belongs to a small teaching temple in Central California. Jerome makes frequent trips to Japan, and in addition to photography, he does koan study with Fukushima Keido Roshi, head abbot of Tofuku-ji Monastery in Kyoto.

Jerome's home and studio are located in the Sierra Nevada foothills near Yosemite National Park. He can be reached at: **www. earthandspirit.com**

We hope you enjoyed this Hay House Lifestyles book.
If you would like to receive a free catalog featuring additional
Hay House books and products, or if you would like information
about the Hay Foundation, please contact:

Hay House, Inc.
P.O. Box 5100
Carlsbad, CA 92018-5100

(760) 431-7695 or (800) 654-5126
(760) 431-6948 (fax) or (800) 650-5115 (fax)
www.hayhouse.com

Published and distributed in Australia by:
Hay House Australia Pty. Ltd. • 18/36 Ralph St. • Alexandria NSW 2015 •
Phone: 612-9669-4299 • *Fax:* 612-9669-4144
www.hayhouse.com.au

Published and distributed in the United Kingdom by:
Hay House UK, Ltd. • Unit 62, Canalot Studios
222 Kensal Rd., London W10 5BN • *Phone:* 44-20-8962-1230
Fax: 44-20-8962-1239 • www.hayhouse.co.uk

Published and distributed in the Republic of South Africa by:
Hay House SA (Pty), Ltd., P.O. Box 990, Witkoppen 2068
Phone/Fax: 27-11-706-6612 • orders@psdprom.co.za

Distributed in Canada by:
Raincoast • 9050 Shaughnessy St., Vancouver, B.C. V6P 6E5
Phone: (604) 323-7100 • *Fax:* (604) 323-2600

Tune in to **www.hayhouseradio.com**™ for the best in inspirational talk
radio featuring top Hay House authors! And, sign up via the Hay House
USA Website to receive the Hay House online newsletter and stay informed
about what's going on with your favorite authors. You'll receive bimonthly
announcements about: Discounts and Offers, Special Events, Product
Highlights, Free Excerpts, Giveaways, and more!
www.hayhouse.com